You Can Draw

Cars

 Gareth Stevens
Publishing

Please visit our website, **www.garethstevens.com**.
For a free color catalog of all our high-quality books,
call toll free 1-800-542-2595 or fax 1-877-542-2596.

Library of Congress Cataloging-in-Publication Data

Bergin, Mark, 1961-
Cars / Mark Bergin.
   p. cm. — (You can draw)
Includes index.
ISBN 978-1-4339-7469-4 (pbk.)
ISBN 978-1-4339-7470-0 (6-pack)
ISBN 978-1-4339-7468-7 (library binding)
1. Automobiles in art—Juvenile literature. 2.
Drawing—Technique—Juvenile literature. I. Title.
NC825.A8B473 2012
743'.89629222—dc23

2011044828

First Edition

Published in 2013 by
Gareth Stevens Publishing
111 East 14th Street, Suite 349
New York, NY 10003

© 2013 The Salariya Book Company Ltd

Editor: Rob Walker

Printed in China

CPSIA compliance information: Batch #SS12GS: For further information contact Gareth Stevens,
New York, New York at 1-800-542-2595.

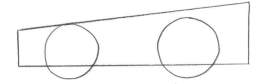

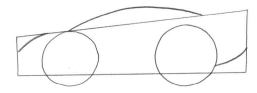

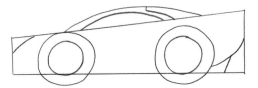

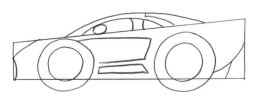

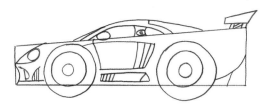

You Can Draw

Draw

Cars

By Mark Bergin

Contents

Introduction

Learning to draw is fun. In this book, a finished drawing will be broken up into stages as a guide to completing your own drawing. However, this is only the beginning. The more you practice, the better you will get. Have fun coming up with cool designs, adding more incredible details, and using new materials to achieve different effects!

This is an example showing how each drawing will be built up in easy stages. New sections of drawing will be shown in color to make each additional step clear.

1

2

3

4

5

With practice, you too will be able to draw cars just like the examples shown here.

Materials

There are many different art materials available that you can use to draw and color your cars. Try out each one for new and exciting results. The more you practice with them, the better your drawing skills will get!

Use a pencil to draw the shape of your car. Any mistakes you make can easily be erased, as can any construction lines that are left over at the end of your drawing.

An eraser can be used to rub out any pencil mistakes. It can also be used to create highlights on pencil drawings.

You can go over your finished pencil lines with pen to make the lines bolder. But remember, a pen line is permanent, so you can't erase any mistakes!

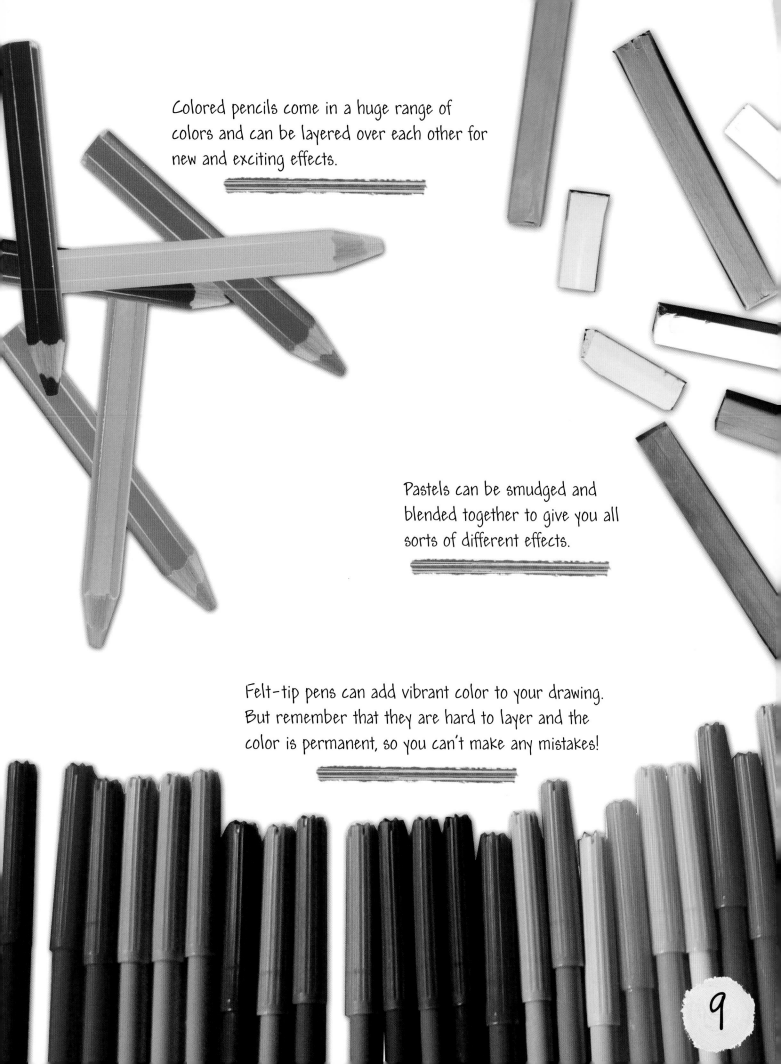

Colored pencils come in a huge range of colors and can be layered over each other for new and exciting effects.

Pastels can be smudged and blended together to give you all sorts of different effects.

Felt-tip pens can add vibrant color to your drawing. But remember that they are hard to layer and the color is permanent, so you can't make any mistakes!

Inspiration

Many types of cars are made throughout the world. You can choose any of them for the inspiration for your cartoon-style drawing. Looking at photos, magazines, or books can give you new ideas and new designs to try.

When turning your car into a cartoon-style, two-dimensional drawing, concentrate on the key elements you want to include and the overall shape of the car.

One way to make your car look cool is to make it a lot shorter in length and make the wheels a lot bigger.

Use new colors and designs to make your car look the way you want it to. It's your drawing, after all.

VW Beetle

The VW Beetle is one of the world's best-known cars. There have been over 20 million produced worldwide.

Draw two circles for the wheels. Add an overlapping rectangle for the body.

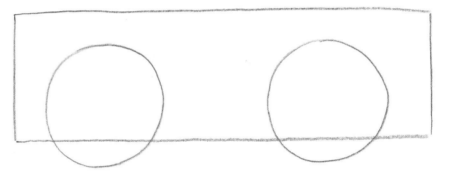

Add curves for the hood, roof, and rear end.

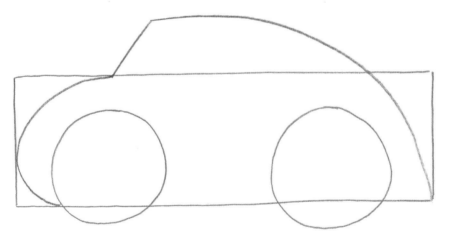

Draw in the front and back bumpers, the wheel arches, and a curve for the windshield.

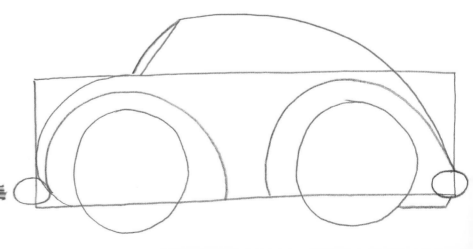

Add two more circles inside each of the wheels. These will be the hubcaps.

Draw in the windows, door handle, and side mirror. Add front and rear lights.

Finish your Beetle by coloring the bodywork. Finish off any leftover details.

13

Bugatti

The Bugatti type 35 was a very successful racing car in the 1920s. It won many Grand Prix races in its time.

Draw two circles for the wheels, with an overlapping rectangle for the body.

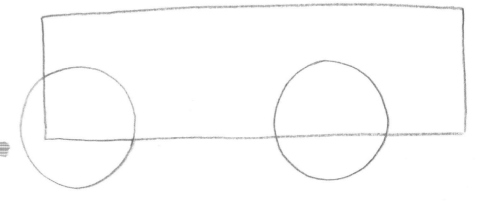

Add curved lines to create the shape of the body.

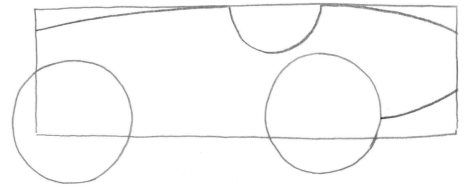

Draw in two circles for the inner wheels and add a spare wheel strapped to the middle of the body.

Draw in vents for the
engine and add other
small details.

Draw in the driver and
add the hubcaps.

Color in your drawing, adding finishing
touches like the racing number.

15

Saleen S7

The Saleen S7 is a very fast road and racing car. The race version has competed in GT championships and at Le Mans.

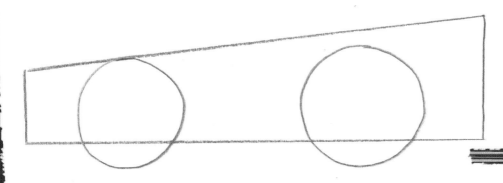

Draw two circles for wheels and add a box shape with a sloping top for the body.

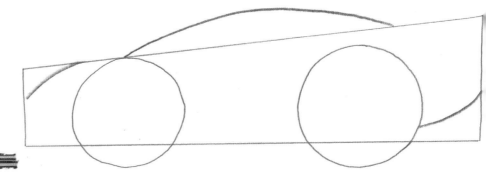

Draw in curved lines to make the shape of the hood, roof, and rear end.

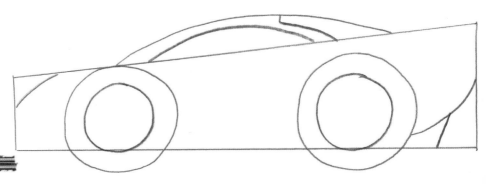

Add the windows and inner circles for the hubcaps.

Draw in the large side air vents and a side mirror.

Add all the remaining small details to the car, such as lights and a rear spoiler.

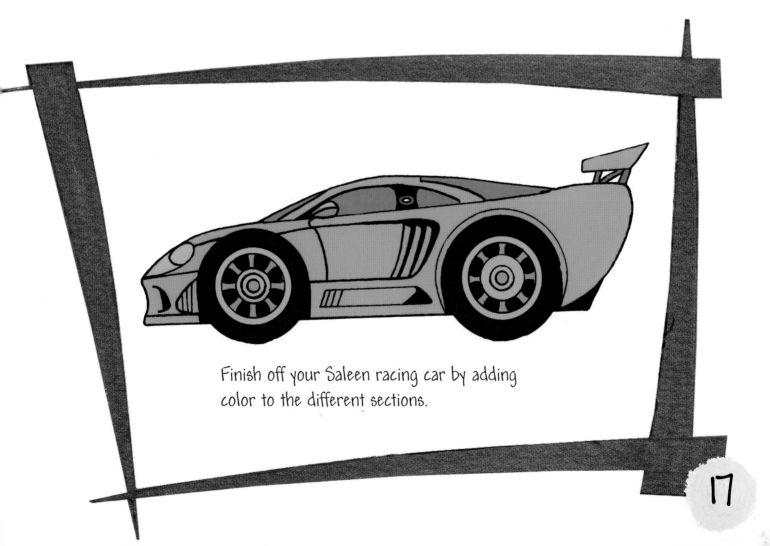

Finish off your Saleen racing car by adding color to the different sections.

Dragster

These cars are designed to compete in straight-line races over a quarter mile (about 400 meters). They run on special fuel and are designed to accelerate incredibly fast.

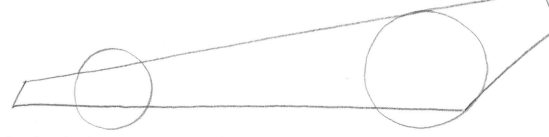

Draw two circles for the wheels; one small, one large. Add the overlapping sloped body shape.

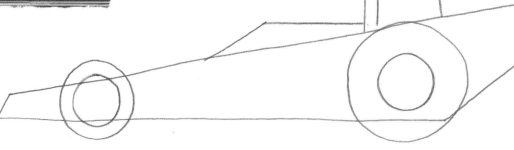

Add an inner circle on each wheel and draw in the driver's seat and the shape of the engine.

Add the driver and the roll bar.

Add the front spoiler, the engine intake, and the rear spoiler.

Draw in the wheel details, the exhaust pipes, and the rear framework.

Color your dragster, adding a racing number and design of your own!

Chrysler

This family car has cool retro styling but all the features of a modern car.

Start your drawing with two circles and add a deep box shape for the main body.

Draw in curves for the body shape. Add the roof and two inner circles for the wheels.

Draw in the roof frame and front and back bumpers, and add circles for the hubcaps.

Draw in the windows and the side mirror.

Draw in the doors and handles, the wheel arches, the headlights, and the tail lights.

Add any remaining details and finish your drawing by coloring it.

21

Cadillac

This classic American car has a really eye-catching shape with massive tail fins at its rear.

Draw two circles for the wheels and add a rectangle for the body.

Add curves for the hood, the roof, and a large tail fin.

Draw in the door and windows. Add the bumper and two lines at the rear of the car.

Draw in the front and rear lights. Add the front grill and draw the wheel arches at different levels.

Add small details to the windows and side of the car. Add more circles to the wheels for the hubcaps.

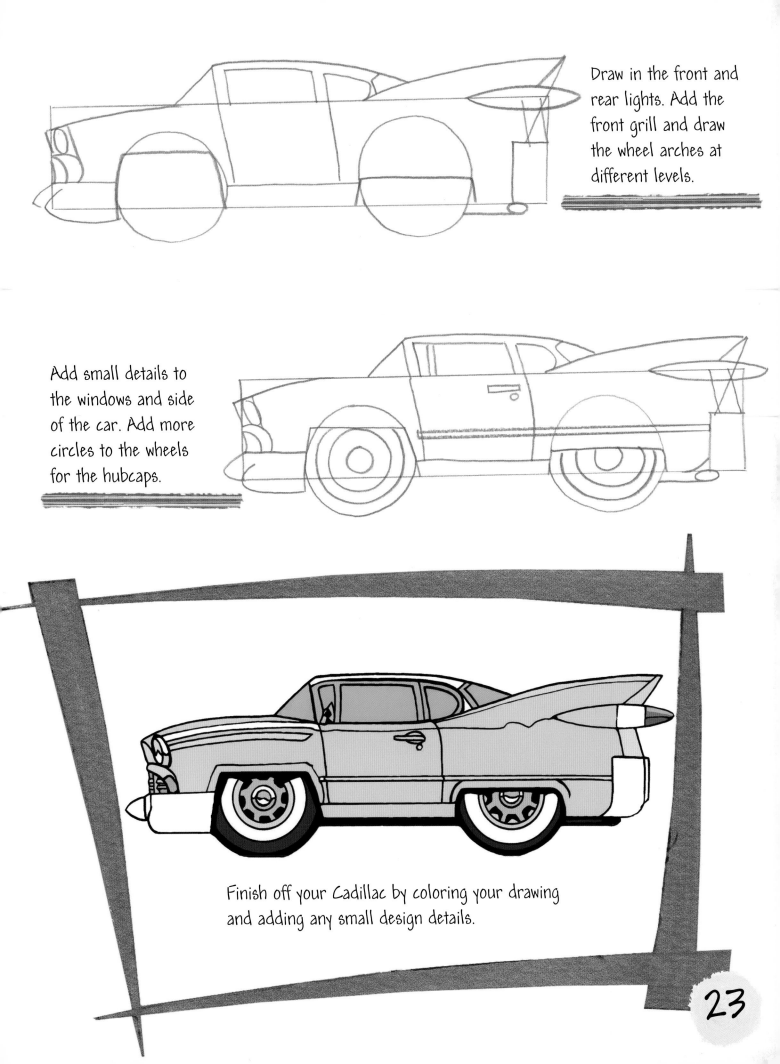

Finish off your Cadillac by coloring your drawing and adding any small design details.

NASCAR

The NASCAR (National Association for Stock Car Auto Racing) vehicle is an American track car built for fast and exciting racing.

Draw in two circles for the wheels and add a long oblong box shape for the body.

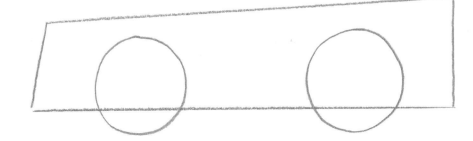

Draw in the shape of the car's roof and the hood dipping inside the box.

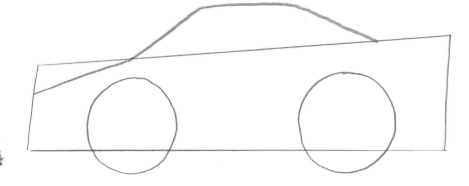

Add the front and rear bumpers and the base of the windows. Add a curve to the front hood.

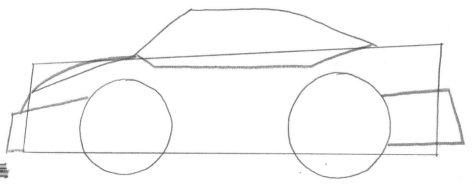

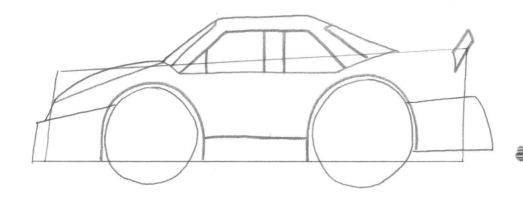

Draw in the windows, a small spoiler, and the curved wheel arches.

Draw in the front and rear lights. Add more circles within the wheels. Draw in the final small details.

Finish off your drawing by adding color and details like sponsorship stickers and the racing number.

Hot Rod

These super-charged street racers are custom built and raced by their owners.

Draw two circles for wheels and add a rectangle shape that is higher at the back.

Add lines for the roof and doors.

Add curves to the body shape and draw in the wheel arches.

Position the windows high in the top section of the car. Add the large engine and the front and rear lights to the car body.

Draw circles within the wheels for the hubcaps. Add lines to the body, and an exhaust.

Finish adding the details of the car and then color it.
Don't forget the awesome fire design down the side of the car!

27

Formula 1

The fastest racing is found in Formula 1. These cars are designed to cut through the air and can reach speeds of 220 mph.

Draw two circles for the wheels and add a sloped box shape for the body.

Add circles within the wheels and a squared-off frame at the rear of the car.

Draw in the front and rear spoiler shapes. Add the driver's helmet.

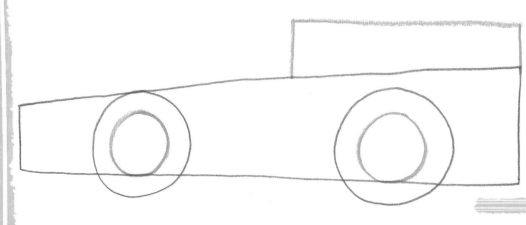

Add more details to the driver's helmet. Draw in lines on the spoilers. Add another small circle in the center of each wheel.

Finish the front spoiler. Add the air intakes on the side. Finish off any remaining details.

Color your Formula 1 car, adding any remaining details and designs you want. Now you're ready for a race!

More Views

For an extra drawing challenge, try drawing your cars from the front or rear! Practicing different views will help you improve your drawing.

Back View

Start with two rectangles for the wheels.

Mini Cooper

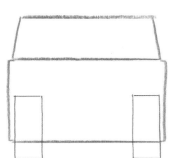

Add another rectangle for the car body then add the rear window.

Draw in the roof, rear lights, license plate, and bumper. Add curves to both sides of the car.

Finish off any details. A pencil has been used to draw and add tone to this example. Try other materials to create a different look.

Front View

Start with two rectangles for the wheels. Add two smaller rectangles as shown.

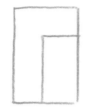

Draw two bigger, overlapping rectangles for the main body of the car.

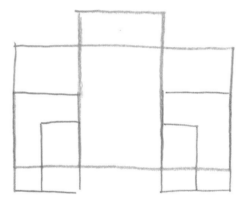

Draw in the windows. Add the front lights and the grill and the hood shapes.

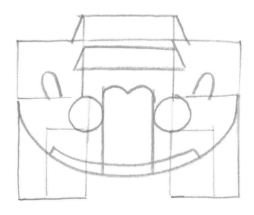

Finish the front view of the car by adding extra details. Then either add color or just add pencil tone as shown.

31

Glossary

bodywork The paintwork on the body of the car.

construction lines Guidelines used in the early stages of a drawing. They are usually erased later.

engine intake A metal tube that's part of the engine of a powerful vehicle.

framework The solid frame that holds the car together and makes its shape.

grill A series of slits in the bodywork, near the car's engine, that help hot air escape.

hood Hinged cover over the engine of a vehicle.

hubcap A metal covering that clips onto the side of a wheel.

roll bar A safety bar featured in racing vehicles. It protects the driver's head in case of a crash.

spoiler A part of the car's design that allows air to flow over the car smoothly.

vent Similar to a grill, but down the side of the car.

wheel arches Arches of metal that protect the tops of the wheels.

Index